Desert Coral

Desert Coral

WATARU MURAYAMA

DESERT CORAL

2

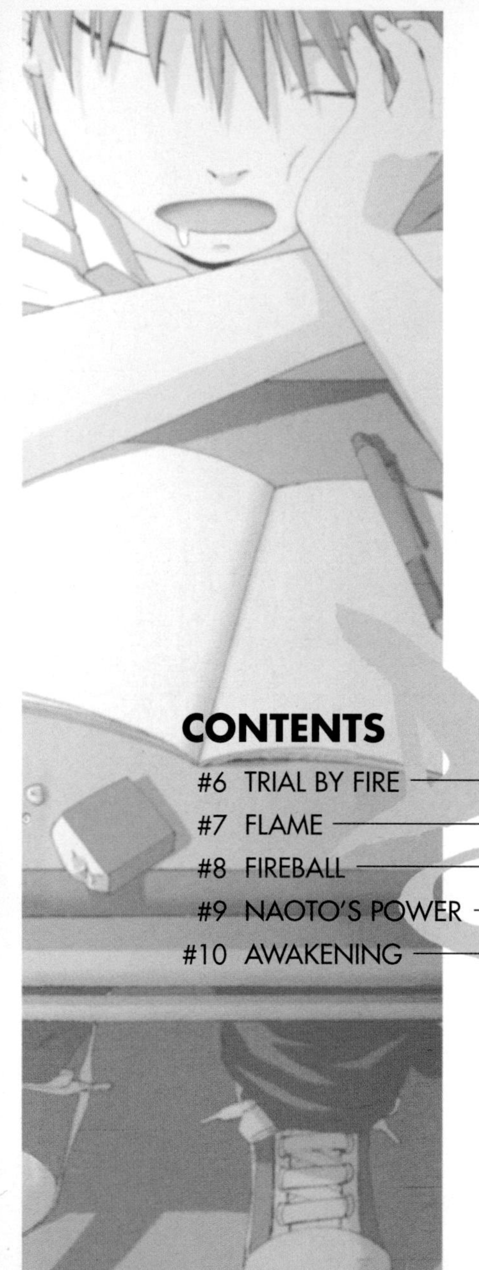

CONTENTS

DESERT CORAL 2

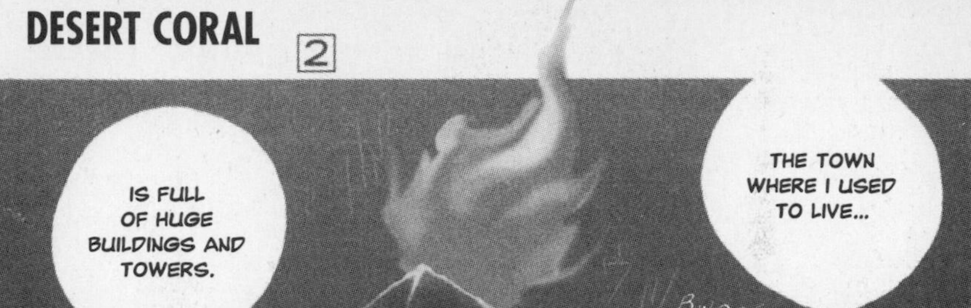

AND, THERE ARE A LOT OF TUNNELS UNDERGROUND.

YEAH, I HEARD!

SOME TRIBES AVOID SUNLIGHT AND LIVE UNDER-GROUND, RIGHT?

THAT'S RIGHT.

BUT IT'S NOT THAT THEY **AVOID** SUNLIGHT.

HUH?

#6
TRIAL BY FIRE

FLICKER
BWHOOF
!
FLICKER
......
WHAT?
IS SOMETHING WRONG?
WHAT WAS THAT?

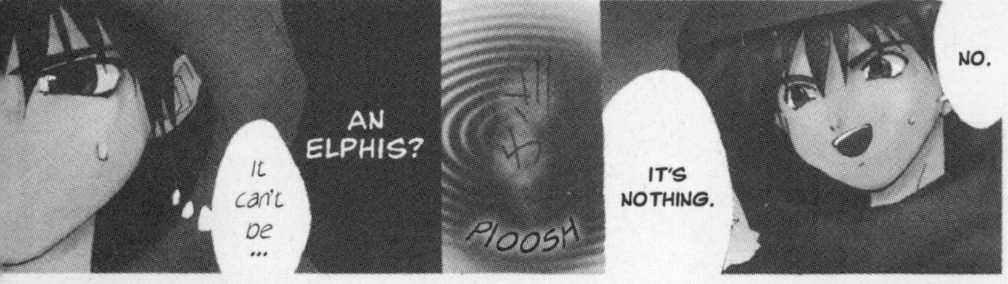
NO.
IT'S NOTHING.
PIOOSH
AN ELPHIS?
It can't be ...

VWOOOR!!!

It's as if it was a world unto itself.

Nobody knows where it is. Nobody knows its history.

It is a mixture of different tribes, languages and customs. The only order is that the sun rises and sets, and the weak yield to the strong.

It exists in a desert at the end of the world, and its name is Orgos.
It's like a box filled with chaos.

There are various other tribes who dwell in the murky shadows of the lowest Region. They are the **Sand Dusts.**

The Elphis is a tribe that resides in the upper Region of Orgos.

chk
BWHOOF
This box of chaos called Orgos is about to be opened.

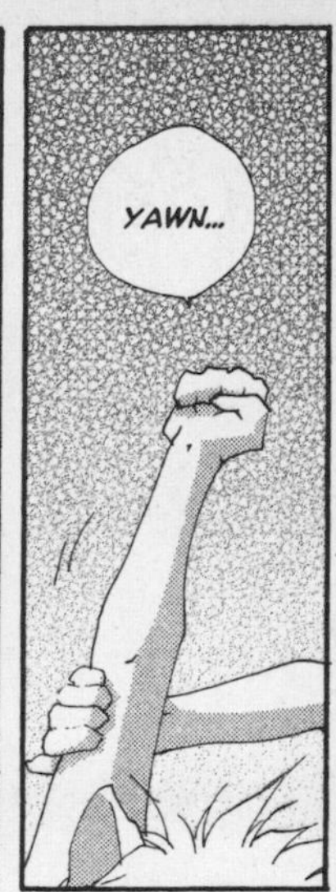
YAWN...

AREN'T THEY FINISHED...
WITH THOSE RITES OF PROTECTION YET?

HERE.
HAVE SOME.
SURE.
IT'S ALMOST OVER. HAVE SOMETHING TO EAT.
Always doin' as he pleases.

sigh
oof
OH WELL...

THOU WHO ART BORN OF FLAME!
WOOO
WOOO
SARAMOOD, YE WHO SLUMBER IN THIS LAND!

I POSSESS THE ANCIENT WISDOM. WE ARE BOUND BY OATH.

I SHALL AWAKEN THEE FROM THY SLEEP.

VGORR

THE ANCIENT WISDOM OBSERVES ALL CHANGE.

THE ANCIENT WISDOM AWAKENS THEE AND SUMMONS THEE.

......

UMM
......

CHATTER
MURMUR
MURMUR

.....
dazed
MAN, I'M BORED.

....
HM?

WHERE'S CAMU, EURO AND THAT OTHER DUDE?!
HELP YOUR-SELVES.
MUNCH MUNCH
UM, YUMMY!
DUNNO.

CAMU'S GONE, AND I'M GETTING WORRIED.
MUNCH
MUNCH
ONE MORE.
PLEASE
YOU DON'T LOOK WORRIED AT ALL.

MUNCH
THUP
I'LL GO LOOK FOR HER.
CHATTER
CHATTER
BWF
YO,

LUSIA...

......
HM

vGOrrrr

CHATTER
RICH FOLK USE THEM TO GO ABROAD.
AND IN THE SKY, YOU SEE THINGS CALLED **AIRPLANES** INSTEAD OF DRAGONS!
ABROAD?
AIR-WHAT?
WHAT DO YOU EAT?

HEY, WHAT'S UP?
YO, NAOTO. ♪
OH, A CAT MAN.

HEY, LEVINAS.

YOU'VE BEEN HERE A WEEK. GETTING USED TO THINGS?
A TAIL!
I THINK SO.

BUT I GUESS IT'S LIKE...
HM?
I FEEL MORE COMFORTABLE HERE.
MORE THAN IN MY **OWN** WORLD.

HA HA.
ぽん PAT
ぽん PAT
THERE, THERE.
TELL US **MORE** STORIES!
Well, I dozed off a lot during class.
NEXT TIME, OKAY?

AWW!
....
WHEN'S **THAT?**
NEXT TIME, I'LL TELL YOU ABOUT WHEN I WAS INVISIBLE.
WHAT?

HEY NAOTO,
I WANNA HEAR ABOUT YOUR WORLD, TOO.

HM. YOU PROBABLY WON'T BELIEVE THIS...

BUT I THINK MY OLD BODY IS STILL THERE, IN MY WORLD.

THANKS TO LUSIA'S POWER, I LOOK REAL IN THIS WORLD NOW.

SMILE

BUT UP UNTIL A WHILE AGO, MY BODY DIDN'T PHYSICALLY EXIST. I WAS **INVISIBLE**.

REALLY?

no kidding

IT'S ALRIGHT IF YOU DON'T BELIEVE ME.

I **DO** BELIEVE YOU.
grin

IT'S BEEN A WHOLE WEEK, HUH?
I GUESS I'VE BEEN HERE ALL THAT TIME.
AND I'VE BEEN UNCONSCIOUS IN THE REAL WORLD...
I BET THINGS ARE PRETTY BAD THERE.

UP 'TILL NOW, I THOUGHT I WAS JUST DREAMING.
......

NOW IT FEELS LIKE THE OTHER WORLD IS...
A DREAM.

....
SCUFF

WHAT'S WRONG, NAOTO?

UH, NOTHING!
WHAT AM I GONNA DO...
IF I CAN'T EVER GO BACK?
I'm so used to it here.

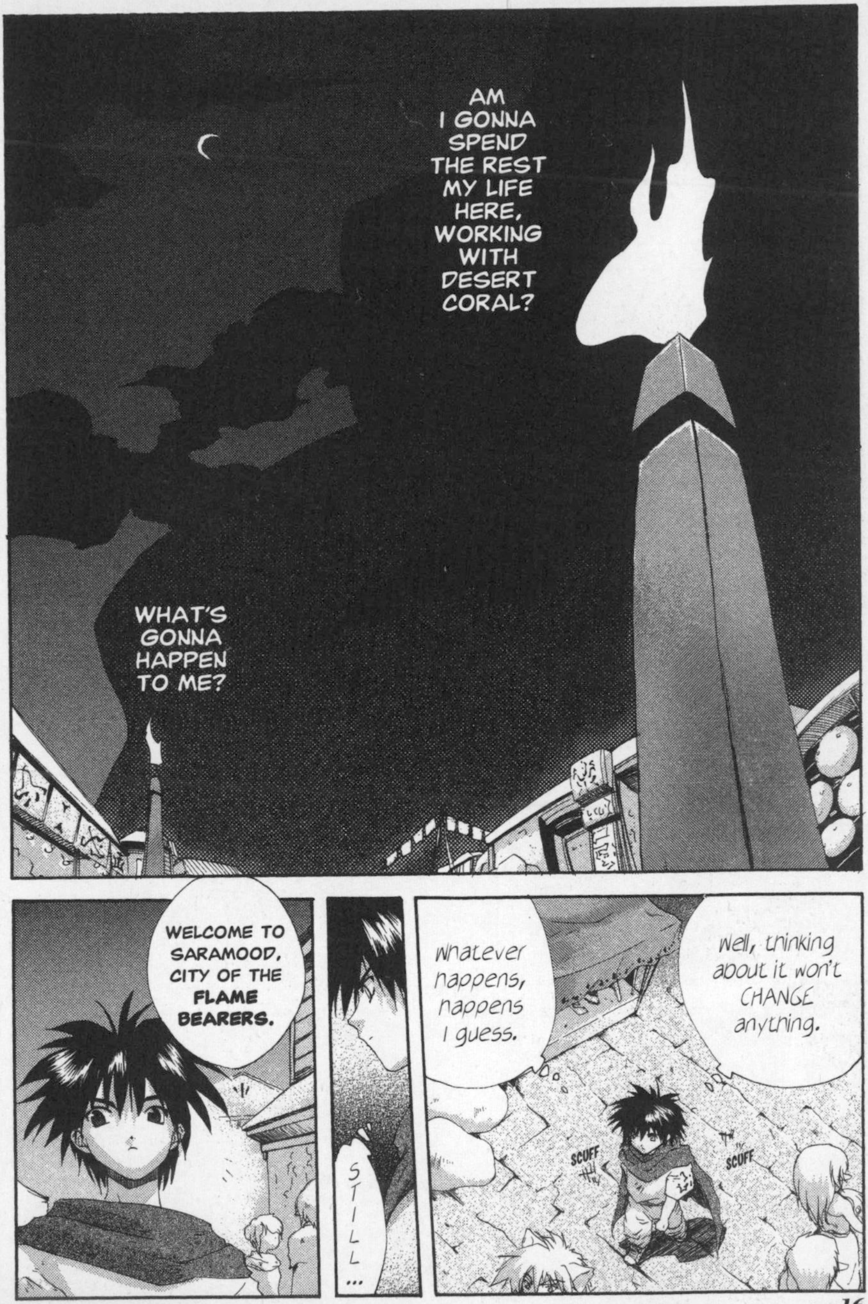

AM I GONNA SPEND THE REST MY LIFE HERE, WORKING WITH DESERT CORAL?

WHAT'S GONNA HAPPEN TO ME?

PLEASE ACCEPT THIS SACRED TORCH...
flicker
OF THE FLAME BEARERS, SARA-MOODALA.
UH, THANKS.
HERE.
OK.
bwoof
Ba-DUMP
?
GRIN
EVERYTHING IN THIS WORLD HAS A MEANING.
IT IS NO ACCIDENT THAT YOU ARE HERE.
ALL THINGS HAVE A REASON AND PURPOSE.

THE WORLD REVOLVES AROUND THOSE WHO POSSESS THE FLAME WITHIN.
BWOOF
?!
MAY THY SOUL RECEIVE THE BLESSING OF THE FLAME.
!!!
THOUGH THE WORLD ITSELF MAY BE JUST AN ILLUSION,
THOUGH THE WORLD ITSELF MAY MERELY BE SOMEONE'S DREAM...
BA-DUMP
BWOOF

HEY.

WHAT'S WRONG, NAOTO?

ARE YOU ALL RIGHT?

......

FWUMP

BOOM
BOOM

C'MON OVER AND WATCH THE SHOW!

ROAR

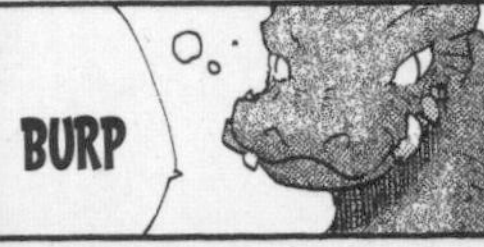

BOOM
IT'S THE AMAZING DRUNKEN FIRE-BREATHING DRAGON!
wa
IF YOU SEE IT, YOU'VE GOTTA PAY!
BOOM
OOOOOOH!
SO BRING OUT YOUR MONEY OR YOUR BOOZE!
wine
HIC

ROAR
yay yay
CAMU!
'yay
HEY, CAMU!
ARE YOU SURE ABOUT THIS?
FIDGET
THE FLAME SPIRIT MIGHT GET MAD! THIS IS A SACRED PLACE!
JINGLE
yay
yay
THE FLAME SPIRIT? YOU MEAN OL' SARAMOOD!
DON'T YOU WORRY. SARAMOOD WILL UNDERSTAND.
HIC
SHE CALLS THE SPIRIT...
jingle
OL' SARAM-OOD?
HEY, DON'T WORRY.
IT'S A FESTIVAL!
HERE GO THE FIREWORKS!
THERE, GIRLIE!
CAMU...
I'M NOT A GIRL.
HIC
ka-BOOM
HYA HA HA
waaa

ぽぽん
BA-BOOM
ほーほほほほ!
Ha Ha Ha Ha!

THAT'S CAMU FOR YOU.
WHAT'S THIS ALL ABOUT?
AND WHAT'S SHE GONNA DO NEXT?

......

MURMUR
......

A BLACK FLAME?
ぼ
BWHOOF

ぽん
BOOM
OOOOOOH!
おおお
WHOA!
It can't be...

HM.
THIS IS AN OLD BOTTLE.
AND IT LOOKS LIKE THERE'S A **SPIRIT** WITHIN IT.

PLEASE ALLOW ME TO INTRODUCE ...
ta-dah
THE SPIRIT WHO LIVES IN THIS WINE BOTTLE.
GROWL
HEH HEH. ♪
O ANCIENT SPIRIT OF THE WINE BOTTLE!
HERE IS ONE WHO WISHES TO BE THY CAPTIVE!
YES!
BWSH

BY THY INCREDIBLE POWER, INVITE ME INTO THY WORLD OF ILLUSION!
WHAT?
?
PNOOF

H-HiC!!
BLUSH
?

AAH... HEY, I FEEL KINDA NICE.
STAGGER

VWOOORRR
THE TIME HAS COME
FOR THIS LAND'S TRANQUILITY TO BE SHATTERED, FOR BLOOD TO FLOW,
THOUGH I PRAY THAT THE LAND SHALL REMAIN AT PEACE...
LUSIA THE BRAVE SHALL FIGHT SO THAT ITS SERENITY SHALL NOT BE BROKEN!

SARAMOOD, SPIRIT OF FLAME!
I PRAY THEE, LEND THY POWER TO LUSIA THE BRAVE!
VWOORRR
!

WHEN MY WISH IS GRANTED, I SHALL...

USE ALL MY POWER TO PROTECT THIS LAND, TOGETHER WITH LUSIA.

GLARE

BA-DUMP

GRANT THY BLESSING OF FLAME TO LUSIA THE BRAVE!

MY BODY IS... GETTING HOT!

CHILD OF THE LUCAVIFATE, THE CURSED ONES...

THE TIME HATH COME FOR THEE TO STAND TRIAL. WHEN THOU HAST OVERCOME THIS TRIAL, I SHALL GRANT THEE MINE POWER.

HOWEVER, SHOULD THE TRIAL OVERCOME THEE, THY WEAK SPIRIT SHALL BE DEVOURED BY THE FLAMES OF HELL.

FLASH

PREPARE THYSELF!!

VWOOORRRR
.....?
SLUMP

WHAT'S THE MATTER?

....

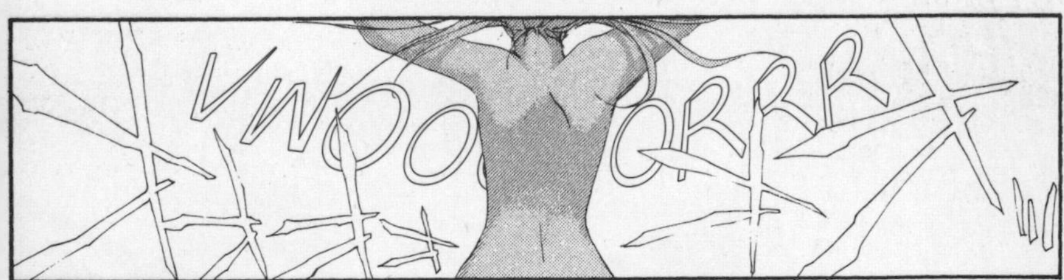
VWOOOORRRR

BWOOOORRR
VWOOM
!!

ELPHIS.
BA-DUMP...

BA-DUMP
HUFF
HUFF
BA-DUMP
BWHOOF
BWHOOF
BWHOOF
BWHOOF

WAIT!
PRIEST!
FWISH
THUP
THIS MAY BE THE **TRIAL.**
HEY, STOP!
LUSIA!
DASH
BLACK FLAMES!
WHAT HAS BROUGHT THIS EVIL ENERGY?!

IF SHE CAN OVERCOME THIS, SHE WILL GAIN THE POWER OF SARAMOOD!!
HOWEVER, IF IT OVERCOMES **HER**, SHE MAY LOSE HER LIFE.
STARE
......
WELL, THERE'S NO NEED FOR YOU TO WORRY!
VWORRR
......
I AM OF THE TRIBE OF SARAMOODALA, THE FLAME BEARERS, PROTECTED BY SARAMOOD! I **CAN** TAKE CARE OF IT, IF NECESSARY.
VWOOORRR
HUFF
HUFF
......
LUSIA...

IT'S SWALLOWING ME!
VWWORRR
HUFF
HUFF
BWHOOF
BWHOOF

WILL SHE BE OKAY?

HEY, PRIEST!

COULD IT BE THE ELPHIS?!

!!

THE EVIL ENERGY IS GETTING STRONGER!

NO. THIS EVIL FLAME IS NOT SARA-MOOD'S.

NO.

IT MAY FAIL.

KA-BOOM

♪ HA HA HA HA!

HA HA

DRINK UP!

HEY, A FESTIVAL!

WHOOPEE

HEH ♪

OOPS, I FORGOT TO PICK A ♪ TARGET FOR MY MAGIC. ♪

#7 FLAME

CHILD OF THE LUCAVIFATE, THE CURSED ONES...
OVERCOME THIS TRIAL GIVEN TO THEE, WITH THY POWERFUL WILL...

ELSE,

URG...

VWORRRR

YOUR BODY...
WILL BE CONSUMED BY THE EVIL OF THE ELPHIS!

THE EVIL OF THE ELPHIS HAS INVADED.
HOW COULD IT ATTACH ITSELF TO THIS SACRED ALTAR?

OH NO!
THE BARRIER WAS NOT COMPLETE!
VGORR

SO THE SPIRIT OF THE ELPHIS JOINED THE FLAME OF SARAMOOD TO CREATE THIS EVIL ENERGY?

VWOORRRR
A SPIRIT THAT CAN'T DEFEND ITSELF AGAINST THE ELPHIS IS USELESS.
HMM...THE STRENGTH OF A SPIRIT DEPENDS ON ITS HANDLER.

LEAVE IT TO ME! I'M RESPONSIBLE FOR THE FAILURE OF THE BARRIER. I'LL DEFEAT THE EVIL ENERGY!

WAIT!

THIS TRIAL IS FOR ME.
YOU STAY OUT OF IT.
BUT ...
THIS HAS GONE BEYOND A TRIAL!
WE MUST DEFEAT THIS EVIL BEFORE CONTIN-UING.

I'LL BE FINE ON MY OWN.

IF LUSIA SAYS SHE'LL BE FINE,

SHE'LL BE FINE.

I HAVE A MISSION.

SWSH

THE LUCAVIFATE BLOOD WITHIN ME IS CRYING OUT, TELLING ME TO FIGHT THE ELPHIS.

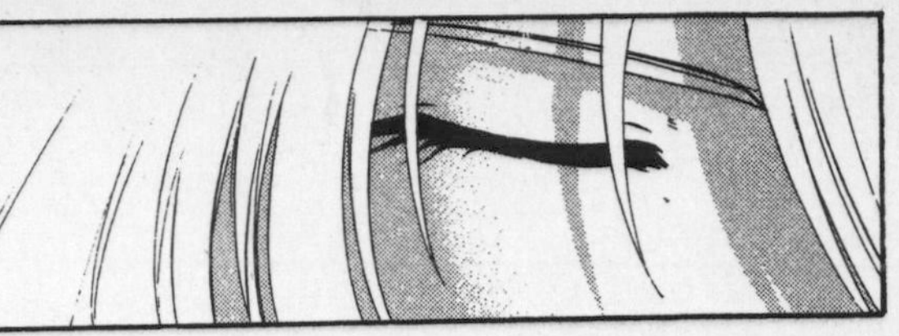

I SHALL FIGHT THE ELPHIS!

THE LUCAVIFATE BLOOD WITHIN ME IS TELLING ME TO KILL THE ELPHIS.

BWF

I...WANT THE FLESH AND BLOOD OF...
THE ELPHIS...
NO!!

KA-BOOM...

crackle...

ONE MORE DRINK!!

CHEERS!

かんぱーい!

GULP

VWOOM

SWOOSH

HUH?

ARGH

SCUFF

LOOM

HEY LEVI. THESE GUYS LOOK PRETTY SCARY.

WHAT?!

STAGGER

LEVINAS! AND NAOTO...

UH, WHAT?

!!
HYAAA
SPLOOSH

SWIP
UGH
OOPS!
SWHIP
WAA!
SMASH

ARGH

The black flames ...
are in them!

THE EVIL SPIRIT OF THE ELPHIS?
AT A TIME LIKE THIS?
SWHIP
THE BLACK FLAMES?
STUCK
THE ELPHIS ARE SPREADING THEM AROUND.
THEY'RE NOTHING COMPARED TO THE MAIN BODY, BUT ONCE THEY TAKE HOLD OF YOU, IT'S HARD TO GET RID OF IT.

THEN WHAT HAPPENS TO YOU?

YOU BECOME A DEMON.
damn

AUGH!

splat
OW!
...
...

WHY YOU ...
THWIP
HOW DARE YOU DEFY ME?!
GLARE
WHAT'RE YOU LOOKIN' AT?
TWITCH
Not again ...
b-dmp b-dmp

POINT
YOU! LUSIA'S SUMMONED MONSTER-BOY! YOUR JOB IS TO FIGHT THE DRAGON!
WHAT?!
YOU SHOULD FEEL HONORED!

GRRR
NOW GO AND FIGHT!
I'M NOT TAKING ORDERS FROM YOU!
WHOA!

CHATTER
LET'S GET OUTTA HERE WHILE WE STILL CAN.
OK...
THP THP
SEE YA!

IF YOU WON'T OBEY ME...

MY DEAR FIRE-BREATHING DRAGON, PUNISH NAOTO!!
WHAT'S WITH YOU?!
WHY ATTACK ME?!
SHUT THE HELL UP!
YOU WERE THE ONE WHO WANTED MY HELP WITH THE DRAGON!

TOO BAD, CAMU.
THUD
No LUSH will beat me!
YOU CAN'T CONTROL THE DRAGON DRUNK.
EEEK!!
ひィイーーッ
...I THINK.
GRRRR
TH-THUD
WHAT?!
LEVI! EURO!
WHIRL
WE'LL ALL WORK TOGETH-ER!
HUH?
WHERE'D THEY GO?!

I'M LEAVIN' TOO!

DASH

HOLD IT RIGHT THERE!

GRAB

ARGH!

SMIRK

DON'T WORRY ABOUT LUSIA. SHE IS WITH THE OTHERS.

YOU'RE RIGHT.

GRR

NOW FOR A DIFFERENT JOB-

PROTECT ME FROM THE DRAGON AND THE PEOPLE UNDER THE EVIL SPIRIT'S CONTROL.

Eeek!

AND DISTRACT THE DRAGON SO IT WON'T ATTACK THE VILLAGERS.

CAN YOU DO IT?

HECK NO!

UGH!

THIS SUCKS!! HOW'D I GET STUCK WITH HER?

Is she friend or foe? Is she even with Desert Coral?

TO TELL YOU THE TRUTH, I WANT TO KNOW HOW POWERFUL YOU ARE.
NOW, GO ON AND FIGHT!
GRAB
YOU CAN'T BE SERIOUS!

IF I WAS LUSIA, I'D SAY...
BA-DMP
WHAT?

FIGHT, MY SERVANT!!
HA HA HA HA HA!
SHUDDER
You ain't Lusia!

SEE YA!
DASH
HEY!

HUFF
HUFF

RRR...
They WERE nice enough earlier...
But now they're after us. Are they possessed?

I'll hide here for a while...

YO.

HA
HA
HA
RR
SHOVE

YO, NAOTO.
GIMME SOME MONEY!
RR...

LET'S GO, CHISATO.
......

RUNNING AWAY, HUH?!
HA HA.
COWARD!

SURE I'M A COWARD! WHO CARES?
I HAVE TO RUN TO SURVIVE!!
I WISH I DIDN'T HAVE TO...

HM.
AN ATTITUDE LIKE THAT...
JUST ISN'T COOL.

WHAT'S MY PURPOSE? WHY AM I HERE?

Always runnin'!

HUFF

HUFF

SORRY, BUT THIS IS THE BEST I CAN DO!

YOU CAN LEARN TO USE MAGIC, TOO, IF YOU WANT.
GRR
THUD
CAMU?
WHERE'D YOU COME FROM,
AND YOU'VE GOT THE DRAGON!
THUD
THUP
THUP
THUP
THUP

BY THE POWER OF SARAMOOD, SPIRIT OF FLAME...
SEED OF FIRE HIDDEN IN MY HEART...
JUST SAY IT!
BY THE POWER OF SARAMOOD, SPIRIT OF, UH, FLAME?
DAMN
SEED OF FIRE HIDDEN IN MY HEART...
GYAAA
OH, WHAT-EVER!
AWAKEN NOW!

?!!
GRR
BA-DUMP!!

GRGH

WHIP

I BET THE **BOOZE** LOWERED THEIR RESISTANCE TO THE EVIL SPIRIT.

IF YOU HADN'T SPLASHED MY FACE, I'D BE LIKE THEM.

THANKS, EURO.

HEH HEH.
BLUSH
I GUESS I **WAS** USEFUL.

I HOPE NAOTO IS OKAY.
I'M A LITTLE WORRIED NOW.
I KINDA DITCHED HIM.
...
THUP
THUP
THUP
THUP

HE'S OKAY, HE'S WITH CAMU.
THUP
THUP
THUP
THAT'S **EXACTLY** WHY I'M WORRIED.

BESIDES...
WE CAN DO WITHOUT **HIM.**

EURO.

thup
LEVINAS,
I CAN'T MAKE FRIENDS WITH SOMEONE LIKE HIM SO EASILY.
YOU'RE FRIENDS WITH HIM JUST 'CUZ LUSIA SAID SO.
....
THAT'S RIGHT.
LUSIA SAID SO.
AND YOU AND I...
ARE FRIENDS BECAUSE LUSIA TOLD US TO BE.
BUT ...
He looks like a wimp.
LET'S GO!
THUP
THUP
THUP
OK.

MY BODY IS GETTING HOTTER!
I CAN FEEL THE ENERGY WELLING UP INSIDE!
FEEL THE ENERGY WITHIN YOU!
AIM IT AT THE TARGET!
IT FEELS INCRED-IBLE!!
AM I COOL, OR WHAT?
RRRROAR
BWHOOF
UGH
He's FINALLY acting like a hero!

HYAAA!
BWF
B-BWHOOF
GO, FIRE BALL!!

GRRRRRR

I'M NO GOOD AT ALL, AM I?

Damn!

HOLD ON!

DASH!

No-good boy,

no-good monster.

CHILD OF THE LUCAVIFATE. CURSED ONES. PATRONS OF CARNAGE!
BE ENGULFED IN THE BLACK FLAME THAT LIVES IN THY HEART!
NO!!
I CAN'T ALLOW YOU TO DEFEAT ME!!

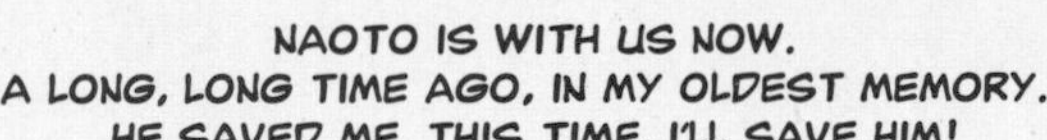

NAOTO IS WITH US NOW.
A LONG, LONG TIME AGO, IN MY OLDEST MEMORY...
HE SAVED ME. THIS TIME, I'LL SAVE HIM!

SARAMOOD, SPIRIT OF FLAME!

GRANT ME THE POWER TO SHIELD ME FROM THE WAVE OF MADNESS THAT STEMS FROM THE DARK!

sizzle

!

Fwhoosh

THE EVIL ENERGY IS VANISHING!

THOU HAST OVERCOME THE TRIAL
RECITE AFTER ME.
ROAR
OOM
!
THUP THUP THUP
HUH?
SUMMONED MONSTER-BOY! WATCH CLOSELY!
WHAT?!
THAT'S THE MAGIC TECHNIQUE YOU MESSED UP EARLIER.

ZWOOO
...
SHE DID IT!
WOW!
scuff
WHAT THE?!

FWOOOOOOSH

W...
WHAT?
What a hangover.
UGH

?
HEY, HE'S BACK TO NORMAL.

THE EVIL SPIRIT'S BEEN PURGED. WE CAN RELAX NOW.
Fwump
SIGH

LOOK
PHEW
LOOK
......
It was not a fire-ball.
ROAR
LIKE I SAID,
THAT'S A SPELL YOU CAN MASTER, IF YOU **WANT** TO.
THUP
THUP

HEY, YOU'RE LUSIA'S SUMMONED MONSTER, SO SHAPE UP!
SHE SAVED YOU THIS TIME. BUT YOU CAN'T ALWAYS JUST RUN AWAY, BOY!
YOU HAVE TO **FIGHT** TO SURVIVE IN THIS WORLD.

I'VE GOTTA GET STRONGER.
ALL I DID WAS RUN AWAY... PITIFUL.

I...
I KNOW THAT!
BUT YOU'RE TOO ROUGH!

LEW.
MOMMY.
......
STARE
WHAT?
MISTER?
THANKS FOR SAVING ME!
YOU...
YOU'RE WELCOME.
YOU CREATE SITUATIONS WHERE WE HAVE NO CHOICE BUT TO FIGHT!
HOW ABOUT ANOTHER DRINK?
HA
HA
HA

LUCAVIFATE... THE SPIRIT OF MY TRIBE BURNS IN THE FLAME OF HATRED.
I CAN'T CONTROL THE LUCAVIFATE BLOOD THAT FLOWS WITHIN ME.
IF I SEE AN ELPHIS, I FORGET EVERYTHING, AND JUST FIGHT.
ボッ
BWHOOF
I LOSE MYSELF, AND DON'T EVEN REMEMBER WHY I HATE THEM.

BUT MAYBE THINGS WILL BE ALL RIGHT AS LONG AS NAOTO'S AROUND.

#8 FIREBALL

I...

I WANT TO FIGHT TO **PROTECT** EVERYONE.

From the darkness...

into the light.

LUSIA, I WILL FOLLOW YOU AND PROTECT YOU NO MATTER WHAT.

I, LEVINAS, PLEDGE MY ALLEGIANCE TO YOU...

FOR AS LONG AS I LIVE.

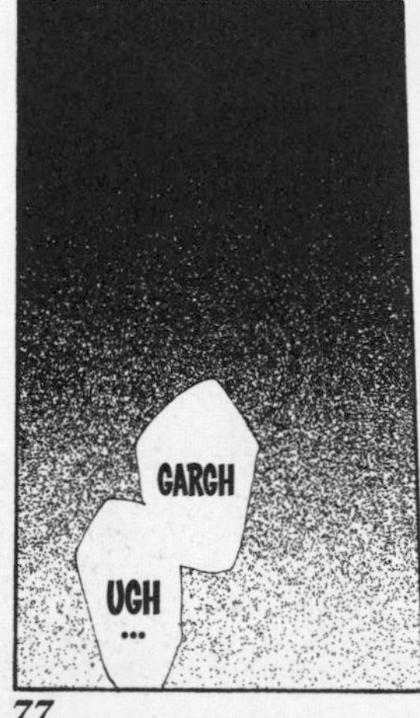
GARGH
UGH ...

HOT...!!

HUFF

WHERE AM I? A DREAM? REALITY?

HUFF

ばっ

!!

FWWSH

AAAH

VWORRR

IT'S BURNING!!!

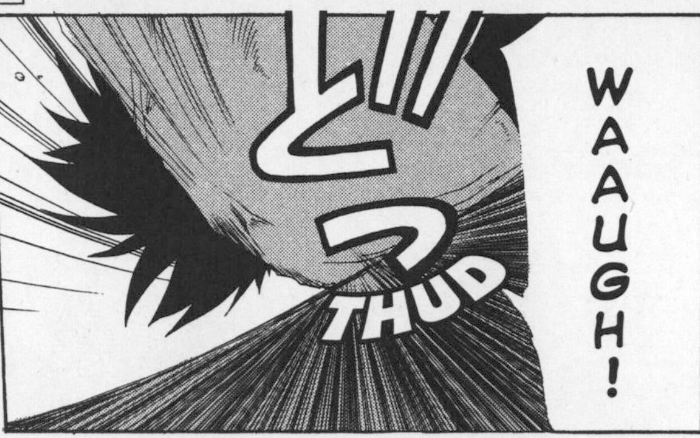
WAAUGH!
THUD

ARGH

bang
bang
bang
HUFF
HUFF
HUFF
A HALLUCINATION?

HUFF
HUFF
DRIP
WHAT'S GOING ON WITH MY BODY?

SLAM
SHUT UP, MORON!
ARGH...

C-
CAMU,
I'M IN ORGOS ?!
GET ME SOME WATER.

IT'S STILL EARLY, SO JUST BE QUIET!

WHIP

......

......

ARCH

I'm in no condition to fight Camu.

...

NO REPLY EH?

HMM. YOU REALLY ARE IN A LOT OF PAIN.

TWITCH

IT'S THE SAME AS WHAT LUSIA WENT THROUGH YESTERDAY, ISN'T IT?

?

IT PROVES THAT YOUR BODY AND LUSIA'S BODY ARE CONNECTED.
THERE'S A TIME DELAY, I THINK. IT WILL EVENTUALLY GO AWAY.

YOUR CASE IS A LITTLE DIFFERENT, BECAUSE LUSIA DID SOMETHING STRANGE.

BEFORE, YOU WERE JUST A SPIRIT, BUT LUSIA'S MAGIC GAVE YOU A PHYSICAL FORM.

WHAT DO YOU THINK THAT BODY IS MADE OF?!

MY BODY?

BA-DUMP

THAT HEAD OF YOURS IS A LOST CAUSE. IT HAS BEEN ALL ALONG.
FIGURE IT OUT FOR YOURSELF, ONCE YOUR FEVER IS GONE.
......
スタ thup
スタ thup

AND...
WHIP
BE SURE NOT TO MAKE ANY NOISE!

ばたん SLAM ...
......

W-WATER...
CAN'T SHE TELL I'M IN PAIN HERE?
SCUFF
I NEED WATER...

LUSIA HAD THE SAME PAIN LAST NIGHT?

I CAN'T...

Why is the water outside?!

WHEEZE

WHEEZE

... POSSIBLY ...

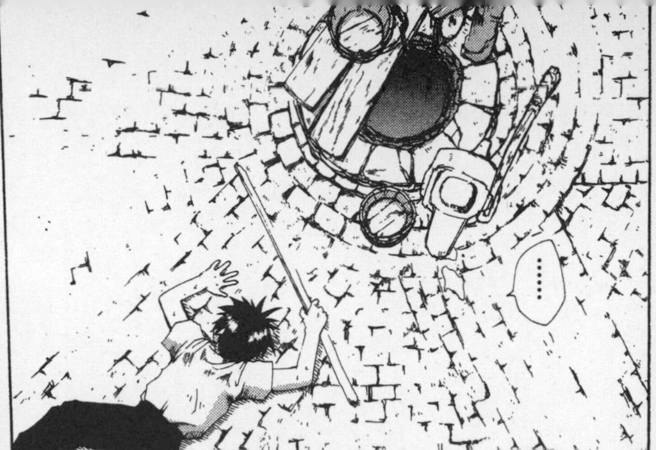
......

TUP

HE'S DEAD!
NOT QUITE.
POUR WATER ON HIM.
水かけてやれ

ざばっ
SPLASH
BWAAH

HE'S BACK TO LIFE!
......
EURO, EPSILON...

splash
ザバ

SLIDE
ズル…

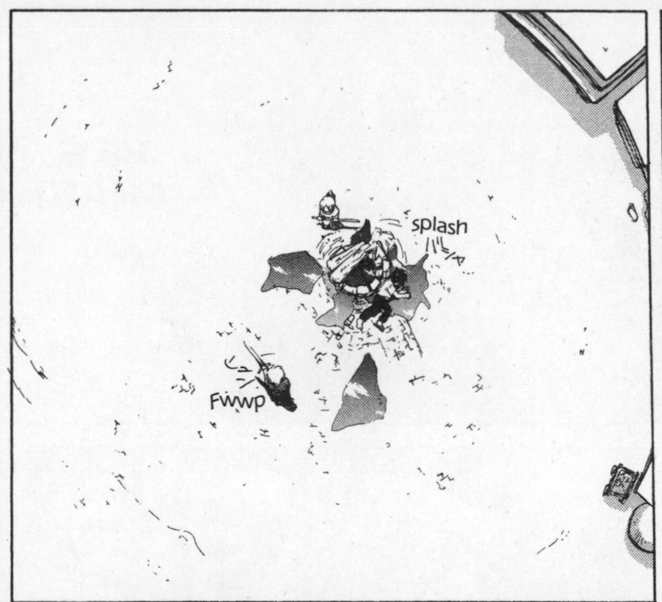
splash
バシャ
Fwwp

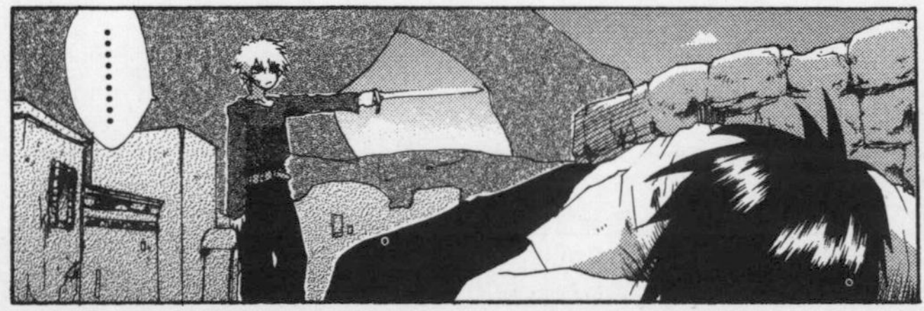
……

DID CAMU TEACH YOU ANY SPELLS?

You want me to help Naoto?
......

LET ME SPAR WITH YOU.

Euro can sword fight?
TAKE CARE OF NAOTO FIRST.

あう wha...

Why ME?
HUFF
HUFF
ARGH
STILL, NAOTO REALLY **IS** IN A LOT OF PAIN. WHAT HAPPENED TO HIM?
......
UGH

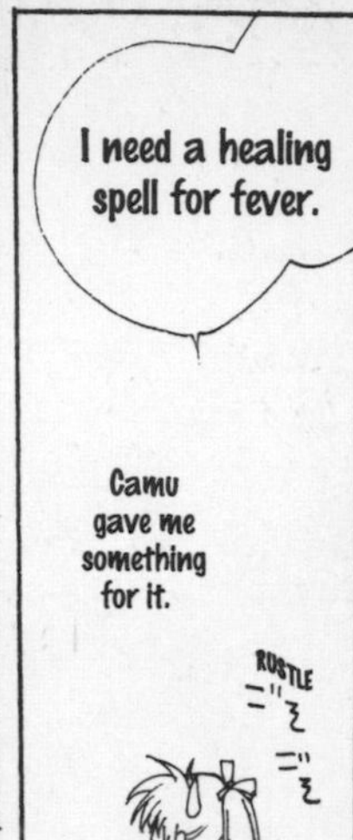

SHEROOT, WIND SPIRIT WITHIN THIS GREEN CRYSTAL BALL.

SEND THE FEVER WITHIN NAOTO BEYOND THE DARKNESS!

NO! NAOTO IS DEAD!
NOT QUITE!

THE FEVER'S INCREDIBLY HIGH...
...
NAOTO!
ARGH

The same as Lusia's ...

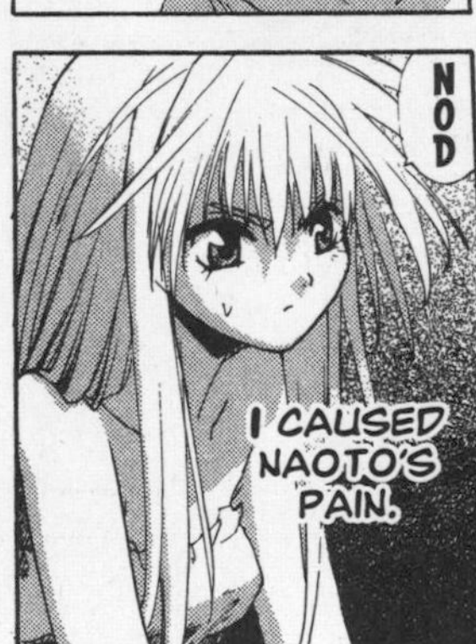
NOD
I CAUSED NAOTO'S PAIN.

LUSIA!

I'LL HANDLE IT!
AGAIN ...

SHHH
ザザァア
COME FORTH FROM THE WELL, AND QUENCH NAOTO'S FEVER!

WART THE WATER SPIRIT, FLOWING PEACEFULLY DEEP BELOW THE EARTH...
!
FWWSH

GOOD.
すくっ
FWP
I won't fail THIS time!

HOW'S THAT?!
I'M SURE IT WORKED THIS TIME!
WELL, HOW IS HE?

がっくし…
SLUMP
WHAT DO WE DO?
umm
う〜ん…

HOT.
UGH
......

LET'S TAKE HIM!
YEAH! I'M SURE CAMU CAN SAVE HIM!
I'm not sure about that!

WHY DON'T YOU TAKE HIM TO CAMU?
!

......

WANT TO LEARN SWORD FIGHTING?
YEAH.

......

THMP
THMP
THMP
THMP
THMP
THMP
THEY'VE ARRIVED.

SLAM
CAMU!
DO SOMETHING!

IS THAT HOW YOU ASK FOR A FAVOR?

BOW-O
FINE. PLEASE DO SOME-THING!
How obedi-ent!

sigh
WELL, I GUESS I COULD HELP HIM.

IT WAS STUPID OF HIM TO GO OUTSIDE!

HE SHOULD'VE STAYED IN HIS ROOM.

DO SOMETHING. HE'S IN PAIN!

NAOTO!

HE IS JUST SO...
PITIFUL!

IT'LL TAKE SOME SERIOUS MAGIC.
THIS FEVER COMES FROM SARAMOOD.
LUSIA, YOU **ARE** AWARE NAOTO HAS THE SEED OF SARAMOOD'S FLAME IN HIM, CORRECT?

nod

I DIDN'T REALIZE THAT SUMMONING NAOTO TO THIS WORLD...
MEANT I'D BE FORCING HIM TO SHARE IN MY SUFFERING.

I'M SO SORRY, NAOTO.
HOW CAN I...

I WILL REMOVE THE CAUSE OF HIS FEVER, THE SEED OF SARAMOOD,
WHICH WILL ATTACH ITSELF TO THIS KNIFE.
SWSH
IT'S BEEN ONLY ONE DAY SINCE NAOTO GOT IT, SO IT SHOULDN'T HAVE TAKEN ROOT. WE SHOULD BE ABLE TO TAKE IT OUT.

Magic stuff sells at a good price.
IT ISN'T SOMETHING
NAOTO CAN'T HANDLE.

UH ...

The best way is probably to sever the thread that ties Lusia and Naoto.

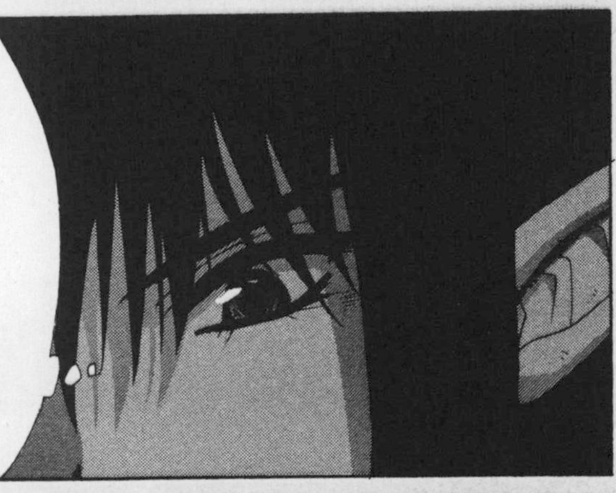

THAT MEANS NAOTO WILL DISAPPEAR FROM THIS WORLD.

I CAN'T HAVE THAT.

LET'S BEGIN.

SARAMOOD, SPIRIT OF FLAME,

HE WHO LIVES WITHIN NAOTO, FIERY SEED OF THE FLAME,

LEAVE THIS BODY, AND APPEAR BEFORE ME.

WSH

ARGH

YOU'RE AWAKE.
!!
NAOTO!
I'M SO GLAD!
EH?
?
fwup
NOW, I'LL TRANSFER IT TO THE KNIFE.
I'll buy a new dress.
waver
waver
HEY!

WHAT WERE YOU DOING WHILE I WAS ASLEEP?
NAOTO?

BONK!

YOU WEREN'T ASLEEP! YOU WERE **UNCONSCIOUS!**

Gargn!!

THAT'S IT!

I'M TRYING TO HELP YOU TO FEEL BETTER.
NOW BE QUIET!

HEAAAA!
FWUP!!
thud
WHO DO YOU THINK YOU ARE, ACTING LIKE THAT?!

HEY! WHAT'RE YOU DOIN'!

AH!

CHOMP

GULP
......!!!
......
......

HUFF. IT'S WHAT LUSIA HAD A TASTE OF YESTERDAY, RIGHT?
THEN I CAN HANDLE IT, TOO.
SIGH

HuH?
He ate it?!
YOU MORON! THAT WAS HARD TO GET OUT!

......
......

flush
I WILL HANDLE IT!

DON'T BE SO NAIVE!

WHEEZE

GRAB

MORON!

WHEEZE

GRAB

!

A GUY LIKE YOU COULD **NEVER** USE MAGIC.

WH...

ARGH

STOP TALKING ABOUT THINGS YOU KNOW NOTHING ABOUT!

"CAN'T KEEP RUNNING AWAY"? EASIER SAID THAN DONE!
IDIOT!

I...
I...
PISSED
GRR

EVEN I CAN HANDLE A FIREBALL.
FWUP
K-CHAK
!

BWHOOF
WHOA! HOT!
FWUP
!!
THUD

I...
I DID IT!
IT WAS A SMALL ONE, BUT...

I UNDERSTAND.

MINE AND LUSIA'S POWER COME FROM THE SAME SOURCE, AND THAT MEANS...

I CAN USE ANY MAGIC LUSIA LEARNS TO USE!

IN EXCHANGE FOR SHARING LUSIA'S PAIN, I GET TO BE STRONGER.

NOT BAD.

I CAN FIGHT.

HE'S USELESS IN A REAL FIGHT.

HANG IN THERE!

DOES HE HAVE POTEN-TIAL?

I DON'T KNOW ABOUT THAT...

UGH

#9 Naoto's Power

SIGH.
WHAT CAN I DO TO BE MORE USEFUL TO EVERYONE?
I'M SUCH A WEAK-LING. ALL I'M DOING HERE IN DESERT CORAL IS...
GROWL!

BEING A BURDEN TO EVERY-ONE.
AH HA HA! ARE YOU WORRIED ABOUT ME?
GROWL
I DON'T UNDER-STAND YOU.
THANKS ♪
THUP

I wish I could ...
......

....

ALL RIGHT! I'M GONNA DO MY BEST!
I'LL AT LEAST DO A GOOD JOB WITH THE CHORES.
cle nch

F-WOOSH
WHAT ELSE SHOULD I BUY?
!
GROWL!

WH-
WHAT?

!!

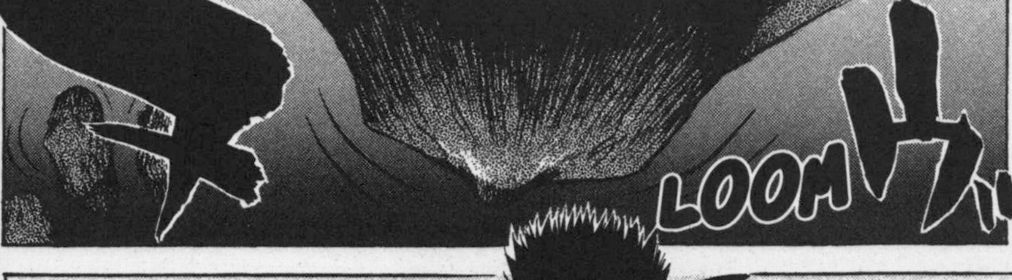
LOOM
HEY, YOU'RE...!!

FIREBALL!
FIREBALL!!
FIREBALL!!!
GRRR
BWHOOF
BWHOOF
BWHOOF
OKAY!!
fwf
fwf
fwf
fwf
fwf
NOW JOIN INTO ONE!!
USELESS!!
しおしおしお～
DEJECTED
失敗
failure
CLENCH
……

LOOKS LIKE YOU'VE MADE A COMPLETE RECOVERY.

You go!
Need more training ...
Should I ask Camu?
Nah.
mumble

HEY, WHERE IS EVERYONE?
IT'S PEACE-FUL WITH-OUT CAMU.

EP AND LEVI ARE WORKING. EURO'S SHOPPING. I DON'T KNOW WHERE CAMU IS.
UMM ...
Really...
FLAP FLAP
So they DO work.

GROWL
A DRAGON.

GROWL
WHAT'S THE MATTER?
YOU CAN UNDER-STAND IT?

NAOTO! THIS IS HORRIBLE! SOMEONE KIDNAPPED EURO!!

DOES HE WANT US TO FOLLOW?

NOD
LET'S GO, NAOTO!

FLAP

THAT'S THE BOY...

I SAW WITH THE TRANS-DIMENSIONAL DRAGON.

AND THAT GIRL IS THE ONE WHO FELL FROM THE SKY.

flip
flip
BWHOOF
HERE IT IS. LUCAVI-FATE.
THEY HAVE SILVER HAIR WITH RED TINT, AND AN ATTRACTIVE PHYSIQUE.
THEY POSSESS EXTRAORDINARY MAGICAL POWER, BUT IT'S LATENT UNTIL THEY ARE TEN YEARS OLD.
BEFORE THAT TIME, THEY ARE QUIET AND DOCILE. IT IS RECOMMENDED TO DISPOSE OF THEM BEFORE THEN.
THEY'RE RANKED 3A...
HMPH...

SARDIS, CAN YOU HEAR ME?

IT BOTHERS ME THAT I CAN'T REMEMBER WHERE I'VE SEEN HER.
I SHOULD HAVE CAPTURED HER BACK THEN.
BWHOOF

THERE ARE TWO NEW PREY. THE ONE WITH LONG HAIR...
I WONDER WHAT KIND OF POWER THEY HAVE.

MAKE SURE YOU DON'T KILL HER.
......

MUMBLE
DAMN. THAT SLAYDIS IS A SLAVE DRIVER.
WHAT DID YOU SAY?

!!!
NOTHING, MASTER SLAYDIS!
GET MOV-ING!
TREMBLE

VWORRRR...
FLAP

A TOWER? IT'S A TOWER?
THAT'S ONE STRANGE-LOOKING TOWER.
FLAP
SCUFF
SCUFF

THIS FEELING ...
IT'S ELPHIS.
MURMUR
MURMUR

WE'LL BE OKAY. LUSIA IS STRONGER THAN THE ELPHIS.

ROAR
?!!

WHY'D IT GET SO DARK?!

!!!
ah

ZWOOOM

WORTHLESS MAGGOTS! WHAT DO YOU WANT IN MY CASTLE?!

ROAR

MASTER SLAYDIS!! MASTER SLAYDIS!!
THIS IS BAD! THIS IS BAD!
SO?

THE GIRL IS LUCAVI-FATE. SHE'S GONNA DEFEAT ME!!
SHE ACTUALLY DID BEAT ME BEFORE.
IT'S ALL RIGHT
IF SHE DEFEATS YOU.
THAT'S CRUEL!
It won't make any differ-ence.
THIS time.
UGH?

HEH HEH HEH... BECAUSE IT'S DIFFERENT THIS TIME. THIS ILLUSION OF ME IS NOT DIRECTLY CONNECTED TO MY REAL BODY.
SO EVEN IF YOU DEFEAT ME, IT WON'T CAUSE ANY DAMAGE.
HMM. HOW UNFORTUNATE FOR YOU SAND DUSTS TO ENCOUNTER ME, MASTER SARDIS, TWICE!

YOU CAUGHT ME OFF GUARD LAST TIME, BUT **THIS** TIME I'M READY!!

Listen to my bluff!

PREPARE YOURSELF!

GWAAAA

SQUELCH

HIS ARM!

I CAN HANDLE THIS BY MYSELF!

NAOTO, I THINK EURO IS IN THAT TOWER.

YOU STAY WITH NAOTO.
OKAY!
GRR

thmp
thmp
thmp

HMM. I DON'T NEED TO DEAL WITH THE OTHER ONE. HE'LL BE EATEN BY MY EVIL MINIONS.
EAT THIS!

HYAA!
ZGROSH
BARRIER!

I STILL...
!!
HYAA
CAN'T HANDLE THE MAGIC YET!
THUD

UGH
BAAM
!!
baWOMP
VWOOrrr
DAMN!
HOOO
EAT THIS!

FIRE-BALL!!
FWAM
!

WAM!

HMPH!!

SCUFF
He shook me off!

BWA HA HA HA HA! WHAT'S WRONG? YOU'RE NOT AS **SPIRITED** AS BEFORE!!
しゅうう
SHOOOMう

BWA HA HA HA
BWA HA HA HA
I'LL WIN!
Now for an Attack Spell!
...

...
swsh
......
WHAT DO I DO?
Forgot the spell.

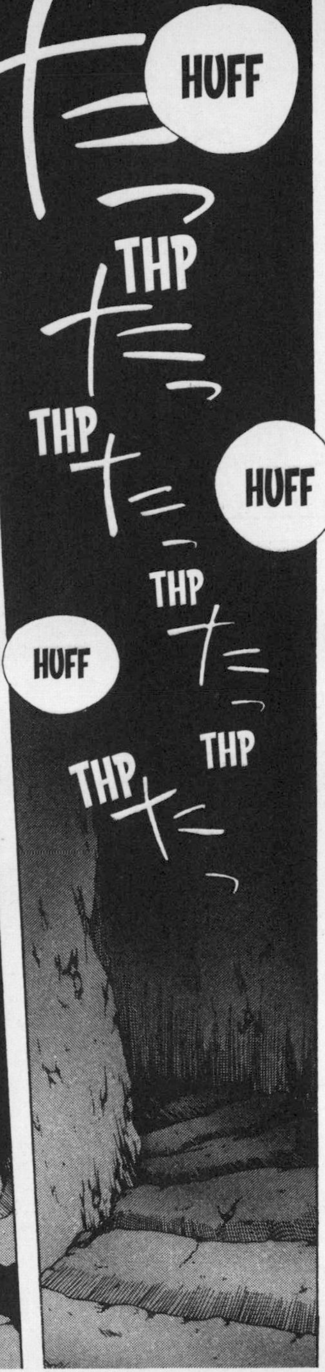
HUFF
THP
THP
HUFF
THP
HUFF
THP
THP

DASH
I GOT OUT OF THE CELL, BUT NOW WHAT?

GRR
!

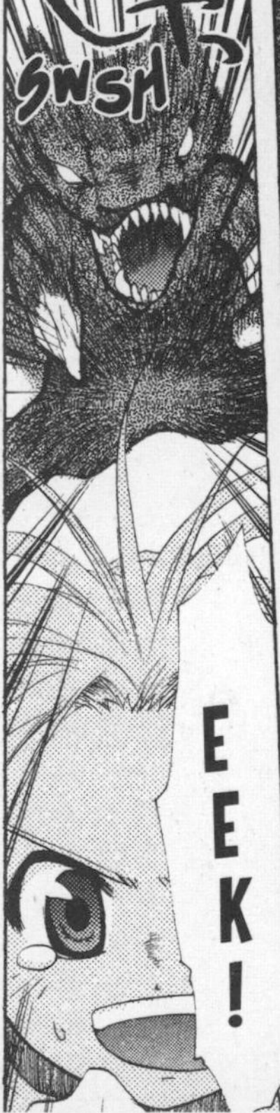
SWSH
EEK!

thup
thup
I CAN'T KEEP RUNNING AWAY ALL THE TIME!
CLENCH
NO WAY I'LL BE A SLAVE TO THE ELPHIS!

GRRR
WHIRL
thup
O ANCIENT SPIRIT ...
OF THE WINE BOTTLE!

FWOOOM
Hope this works on monsters.
HERE IS ONE WHO WISHES TO BE THY CAPTIVE!
BY THY INCREDIBLE POWER,
VWOOORR
INVITE MINE ENEMY INTO THY WORLD OF GHOSTLY ILLUSION!

pwhoof
IT WORKED!
Camu forgot "mine enemy."

SCUFF
!

SHOOM
WAAA!

DAMN!
I SEE. THERE WAS MORE THAN ONE OF THEM!!

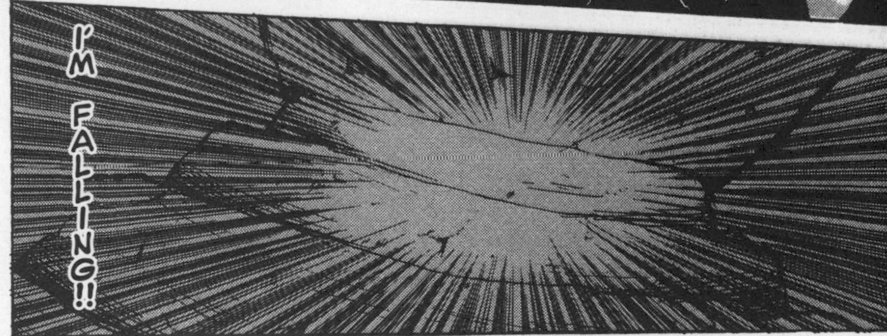
I'M FALLING!!

THUD
UGH!

klunk

WAAA
FWIP

THE MAGIC ROCK I GOT EARLIER. IF I COULD SMASH IT...

GRARR
!

I'M DONE FOR.
I DON'T EVEN HAVE ENOUGH STRENGTH TO SMASH THIS ROCK.
SNIFFLE

FLAP
GRR
GRRR
SGROK
GYAA?!
THUP
EURO, THIS WAY!!
RUN!!
?!
GRR
dash
GRAB
HURRY! RUN!
NAOTO?
WHY'RE YOU HERE?!

GUAAA
THMP
THMP
THMP
HUFF
HUFF
HUFF

FWWSH
WHAT THE?!
WHY THE HECK ARE YOU HERE, NAOTO?!

SORRY.
I CAME WITH LUSIA TO RESCUE YOU.

BLUSH
WHA...

I...
I DON'T WANT YOU TO RESCUE ME!!

YEAH! IF I'D TRIED A BIT HARDER, I COULD'VE GOTTEN AWAY ON MY OWN.

I CAN'T EVEN BEAT AN ELPHIS.

BUT I GOT **RESCUED** BY **NAOTO!**

CLENCH

......!
WHERE'S LUSIA?

....
SHE'S FIGHTING WITH AN ELPHIS OUTSIDE.
I'M SURE SHE'LL BEAT IT AND COME LOOKING FOR US.
They really DO hate me.

WE'VE GOTTA HURRY AND RESCUE HER!

?

LUSIA IS DIFFERENT NOW!!

SHE'S FIGHTING WITH HER POWER SEALED!!

WHAT DO YOU MEAN?
Lusia said she would be all right.

I'VE GOTTA HURRY AND SMASH THIS.
WHAT'S THAT?

IT'S A **DEMONIC POWER STONE.** IT'S THE SOURCE OF THE ELPHIS'S MAGIC POWER.
ONCE WE CRUSH THIS, THE ILLUSION OF THAT ELPHIS WILL DISAPPEAR!

WHERE DID YOU GET THAT?
I WASN'T JUST SITTING AROUND WHEN I GOT CAUGHT. I SNATCHED THIS WHEN I ESCAPED.

THE ELPHIS LUSIA IS FIGHTING NOW ISN'T REAL. IT'S AN ILLUSION, JUST LIKE BEFORE.
THE REAL ELPHIS RARELY COMES DOWN HERE.
WHAT'S DIFFERENT THIS TIME IS THAT THE SOURCE OF THE MAGIC IS THIS DEMONIC POWER STONE, NOT THE REAL ELPHIS.
HMM. I DON'T UNDER-STAND.

AND...
THERE ARE THREE WAYS TO BEAT IT.

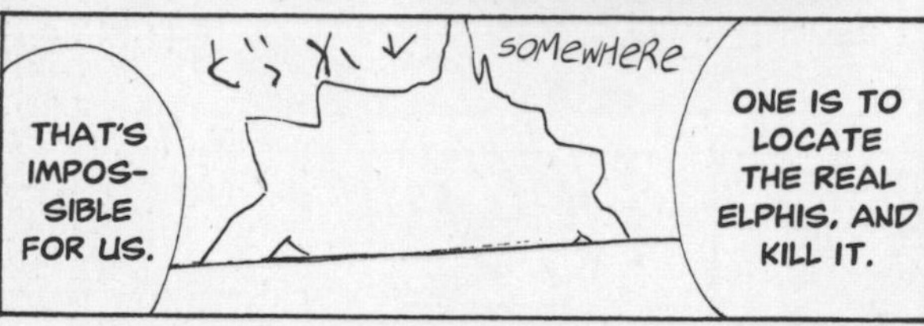
ONE IS TO LOCATE THE REAL ELPHIS, AND KILL IT.
SOMEWHERE
THAT'S IMPOS-SIBLE FOR US.

THE SECOND IS TO GET RID OF ALL THE ILLUSIONS LIKE LUSIA DID BEFORE.
YAH
ZAP
BUT THEY'LL ALL REAPPEAR.

THE LAST IS TO CRUSH THIS DEMONIC POWER STONE!
BUT...

nod
YOU CAN'T, RIGHT?

FLAP
THEN WE'LL HAVE TO RELY ON LUSIA.

I TOLD YOU, SHE CAN'T BEAT HIM...
WITH-OUT THE POWER OF THE LUCAVI-FATE.

......
WHAT HAPPEN-ED TO HER?

DUNNO! BUT EVER SINCE YOU CAME...

LUSIA HASN'T BEEN THE SAME. IT'S ALL YOUR FAULT!!

WHY WOULD THE LIKES OF **YOU** BE SO "SPECIAL" TO HER?!

EURO ...

ARE YOU BY ANY CHANCE... I MEAN...

YOU **ARE** A GIRL, RIGHT?

......

blush

BWF

WATCH OUT.
? WHO'S THERE?
YOU'RE ONLY AN ILLUSION, TOO. YOUR REAL SELF IS SOMEWHERE ELSE.
EVEN IF I WIPE YOU OUT, YOU'D JUST GO BACK TO YOUR OTHER WORLD.
NO MATTER HOW STRONG YOUR SPIRIT IS, THE ELPHIS'S POWER STONE WILL CONSUME YOU WITH ITS EVIL.
NOW WAIT JUST A MINUTE, EURO!

VWOOORRR
SCUFF
SCUFF

Damn. What do I do now?!

POWER ...
!
SHOW ME YOUR POWER!

?
Who's that?

SHOW ME HOW YOU RELEASE YOUR POWER!!

THE POWER OF THE LUCAVIFATE!
BA-DUMP
NO!!

THUD
DASH

!!

SHADOW!!

LOOM
GRAB

I GOT HER!
WAAA!
DANGLE

HEH HEH HEH. THAT WAS **TOO** EASY!
ARGH!

HMM.

fwup

IS THAT **REALLY** ALL THERE IS TO THE POWER OF LUCAVIFATE?

#10 AWAKENING

NAOTO, I WILL...

SEND YOU BACK TO YOUR WORLD!

I WILL DEFEAT YOU! LEAVE THIS WORLD!!
ぼぅっ
BWHOOF

EURO, THAT SPIRIT IS OVER-POWERING YOU!
THROW THE ROCK DOWN, QUICKLY!!

くら
totter
HUNH ...

SHADDUP!
バチッ
Bwof

GRAARG
GRRRRRR
!!!
GRR
GRRRRRRR

THE ONLY FIGHTING TECHNIQUE I HAVE IS THAT USELESS FIREBALL.

HOW AM I GONNA FIGHT?

Should I punch her?

WHY **ARE** YOU HERE?! WHY DID YOU COME?!

NEITHER OF US SHOULD BE HERE!!

BECAUSE LUSIA CALLED ME.

BECAUSE LUSIA NEEDS ME.

WHY?

AM I DOING WHAT SHE WANTED ME TO DO? IT'S NOT LIKE I CAN DO ANYTHING ANYWAY. WHY **AM** I HERE?

WHY'RE YOU SAYING THAT? WHAT ABOUT **YOU**.

WHY'RE YOU IN DESERT CORAL...

EURO?

FSHHHH

WHY IS EURO HERE?

I...
I...

FROM NOW ON, YOU'RE ONE OF US!

HUP

GRR

SORRY, BUT I JUST **CAN'T** FIGHT YOU.

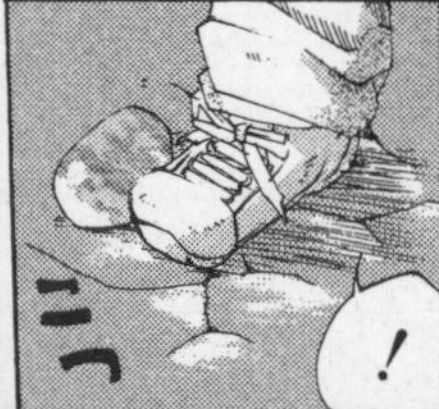

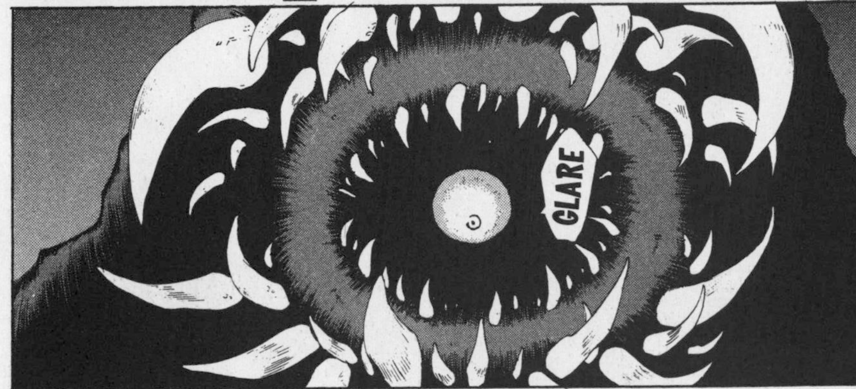
GLARE

FOR NOW, WE GOTTA GET OUT OF HERE!
peek
DASH
GROWL
GRR
RUNNING, HUH?
SIGH. WHY ME?! WHAT AM I EVEN DOING HERE?

I WISH I COULD WAKE UP.
THUP
THUP
THUP
UNGH... NAOTO.
DON'T WORRY,
I'M USED TO THIS NOW.
THUP
THUP

GARGH

?!!

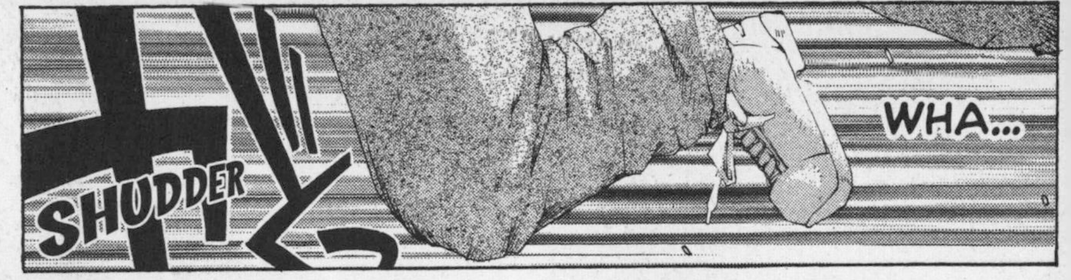
WHA...
SHUDDER

WHAT THE HECK?! WHAT'S HAPPEN-ING?!
SCUFF
HUFF
THWOP
?!
NAOTO?!

IT HURTS!! I CAN'T BREATHE!!
HUFF
HUFF

LUSIA!!

THIS PAIN IS LUSIA'S.

SO DOES THAT MEAN **SHE'S** UNDER ATTACK?!

GAARGH

ARGH
UGH
NAOTO!!

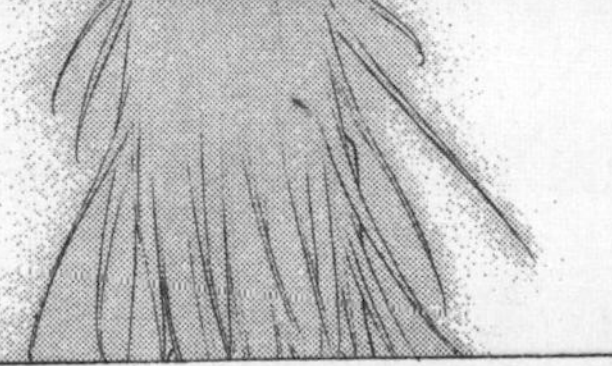
LUSIA!
SHE SAID SHE WOULD BE ALL RIGHT!

EURO, WE HAVE TO HURRY.
LUSIA IS BEING ATTACK-ED!

?!

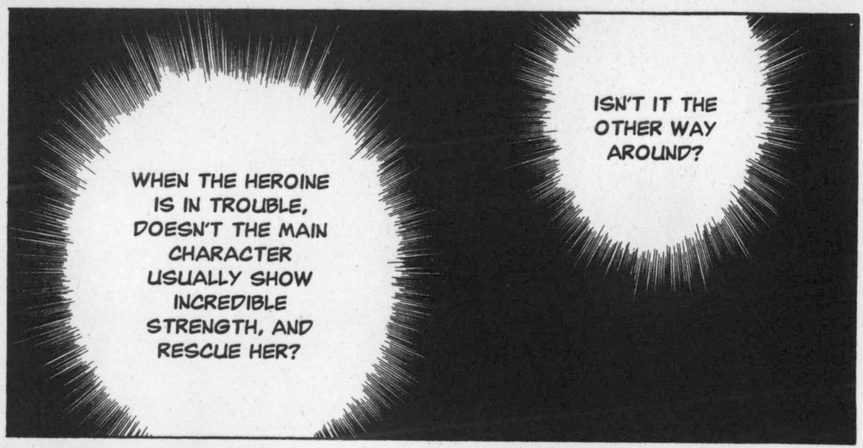

THE ANSWER IS SIMPLE, BOY. IF YOU CAN'T OVERCOME THIS, YOU DON'T DESERVE TO BE THE MAIN CHARACTER IN THIS WORLD.

ばっ

FWUP

UGH

SHADDUP!!

HYAA

BWHOOF

fwup

BWHOOF

WHOSE VOICE IS IN MY HEAD?!

...

IF YOU HAVE **THAT** MUCH SPIRIT LEFT, YOU MUST BE ALRIGHT.

L'SKSH

GRR

......

GRRR

SHOW ME WHAT YOU'VE GOT, AND I DON'T MEAN THAT MISERABLE FIREBALL MAGIC.

SHOW ME YOUR **OWN** POWER!

DAMN. WHAT DO I DO?
THE ONLY THING I CAN DO IS TRAVEL BETWEEN THE REAL WORLD AND ORGOS.

YES. LIKE THE DIMENSIONAL DRAGON!

LISTEN, BOY. DRAGONS ARE THE EMBODIMENT OF THE GODS. THE DIMENSIONAL DRAGON IS LIKE AN ALMIGHTY GOD RULING OVER TIME AND SPACE.

IF THERE'S SOMETHING YOU DESIRE, MERELY FORM ITS IMAGE IN YOUR MIND, AND IT IS YOURS!

NOW, WHAT IS IT YOU WANT?

Something to defeat these demons.
GULP

RIGHT!
BWHOOF

ZWOOSH
A SWORD!
I WANT A SWORD!!

VWOORRRR
HYAAAAA!

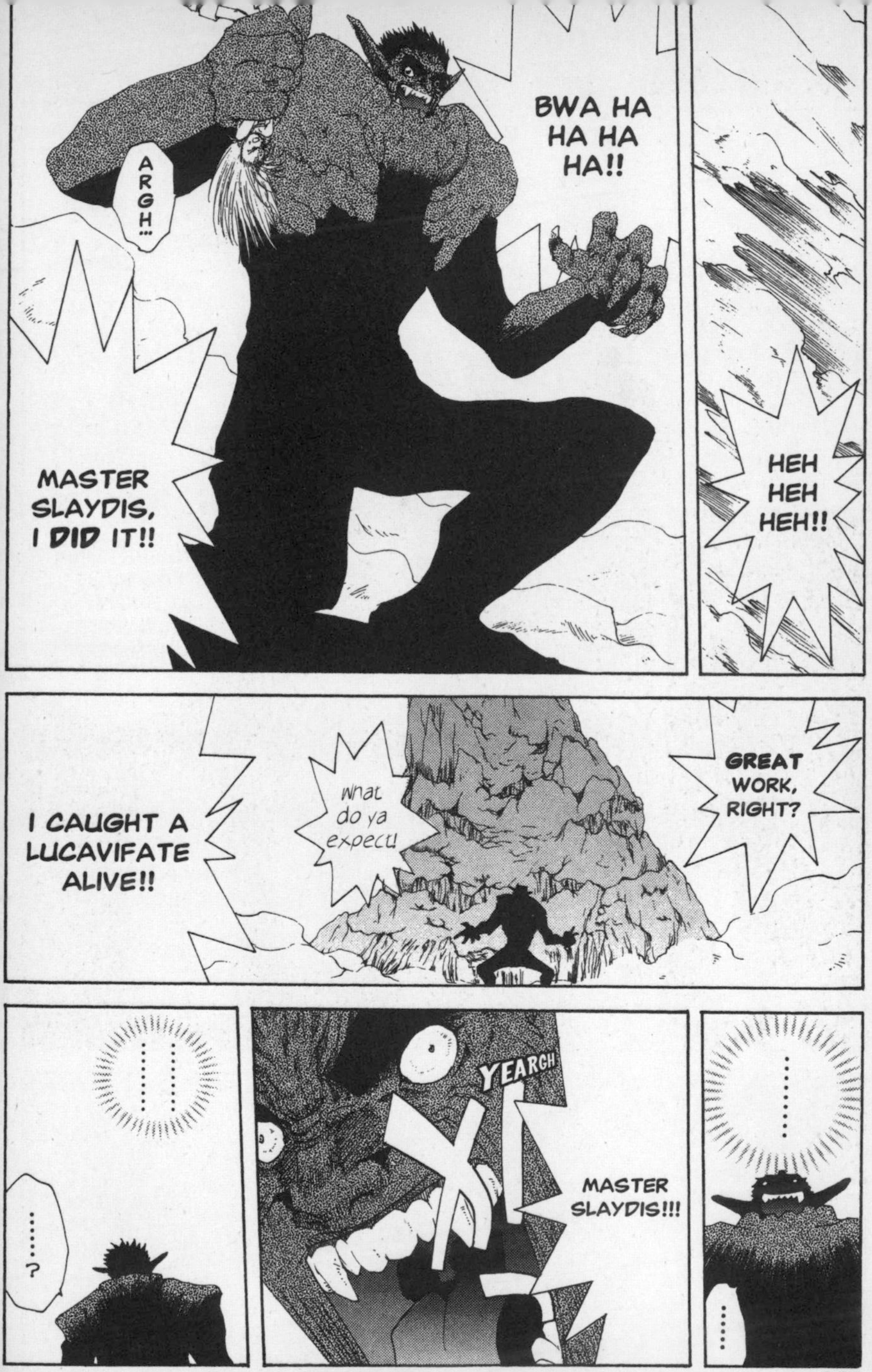

ARGH...
BWA HA HA HA HA!!
MASTER SLAYDIS, I DID IT!!
HEH HEH HEH!!

I DON'T NEED IT ANY MORE.
HUH?

DO WHATEVER YOU WANT WITH IT. I'M NO LONGER INTERESTED.
WHAT?!
I'M MUCH MORE INTERESTED IN THE BOY WHO'S CONNECTED TO THE DIMENSIONAL DRAGON.

BYE NOW.
CLICK
H-HEY! WAIT A MINUTE

THUD
!

......
?
FWWSH
DAMN YOU, SLAY-DIS.

GLARE
HMPH. OH WELL.
I GUESS IT DOESN'T MATTER. BECAUSE NOW I GET TO KILL HER.

...

WE **WON'T** LET YOU!

CAMU!
LEVI!
SCUFF

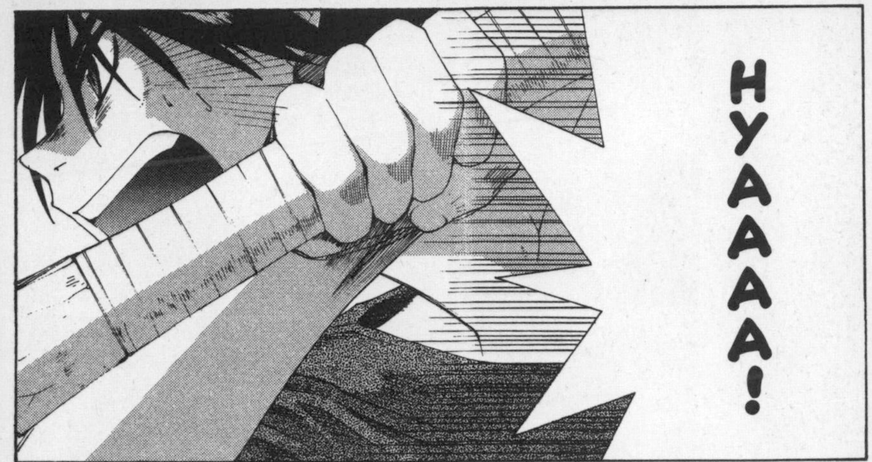
HYAAAAA!

THIS IS THE LAST ONE!
THWASH
GYAAAA

N-
NAOTO IS FIGHTING.

HUFF
HUFF
HUFF
SCHOOOM
.....
...

WITH MY NEW POWER, MAYBE I CAN CRUSH...
TWITCH
THE POWER STONE!

OH YEAH!
HUH?

DON'T TOUCH THAT!
ずざざっ
SCUFF SCUFF
WHAT? WE CAN'T RESCUE LUSIA WITHOUT IT.
BESIDES, YOU'RE THE ONE WHO BROUGHT THE THING.

Holding it doesn't affect him?

I'M GOING TO CRUSH THIS ROCK!!
BUT HOW?

I KNOW!
SMILE
I KNOW WHY MY FIRE-BALLS WERE SO SMALL!
BWHOOF
GRAB
GRAB
I CAN HAVE ANY-THING I IM-AGINE.
BUT JUST TRYING TO VISUAL-IZE IT IS **NOT** ENOUGH.
I HAVE TO USE MY FIRE-BALL TO MAKE IT REAL!!

YES.
THE FLAME IS THE SOURCE OF EVERY-THING.
SO, HE REALLY **ISN'T** JUST AN ORDINARY BOY.

ta-dah
THAT'S HEAVY!
I DID IT!
A HAMMER!
!!

BWA
HA
HA
HA!!
VWOORRR
IT DOESN'T MATTER HOW MANY SAND DUSTS THERE ARE!

I'VE SEEN ENOUGH.
THANKS FOR A GOOD SHOW.
SNAP

CRACK

BAAM
ARGH!
CRACK
CRACK

GAARGH
?!!
crumble
W-WAIT A MINUTE!! MASTER SLAYDIS?!

AAAH!!
......
WE DIDN'T EVEN DO ANYTHING!

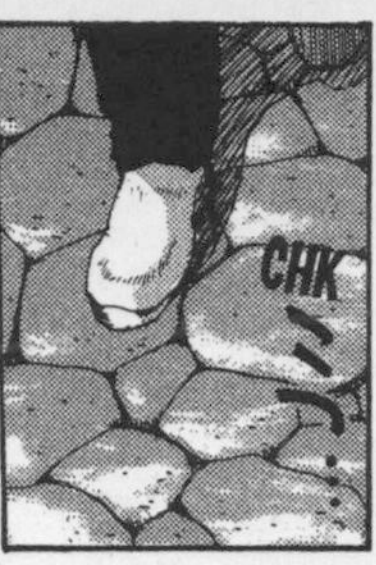

NAOTO.

SO YOU'VE FINALLY **AWAKENED?**

L-LOOKS LIKE IT!
CLAP
ぱん!

EURO! YOU DID IT!
WE MADE IT!
PAT
FLAP
GRRR
WOW
......

Y-YEAH ...
BUT... I...
BUT... I...

......

LET'S HURRY. EVERYONE'S WAITING FOR US.
!
......

I-I'VE GOTTA APOLOGIZE!
BOW
B O W
NAOTO! I-I'M SORRY...

LET'S GO HOME.

OK. ♡

DESERT CORAL 2 END

Desert Coral

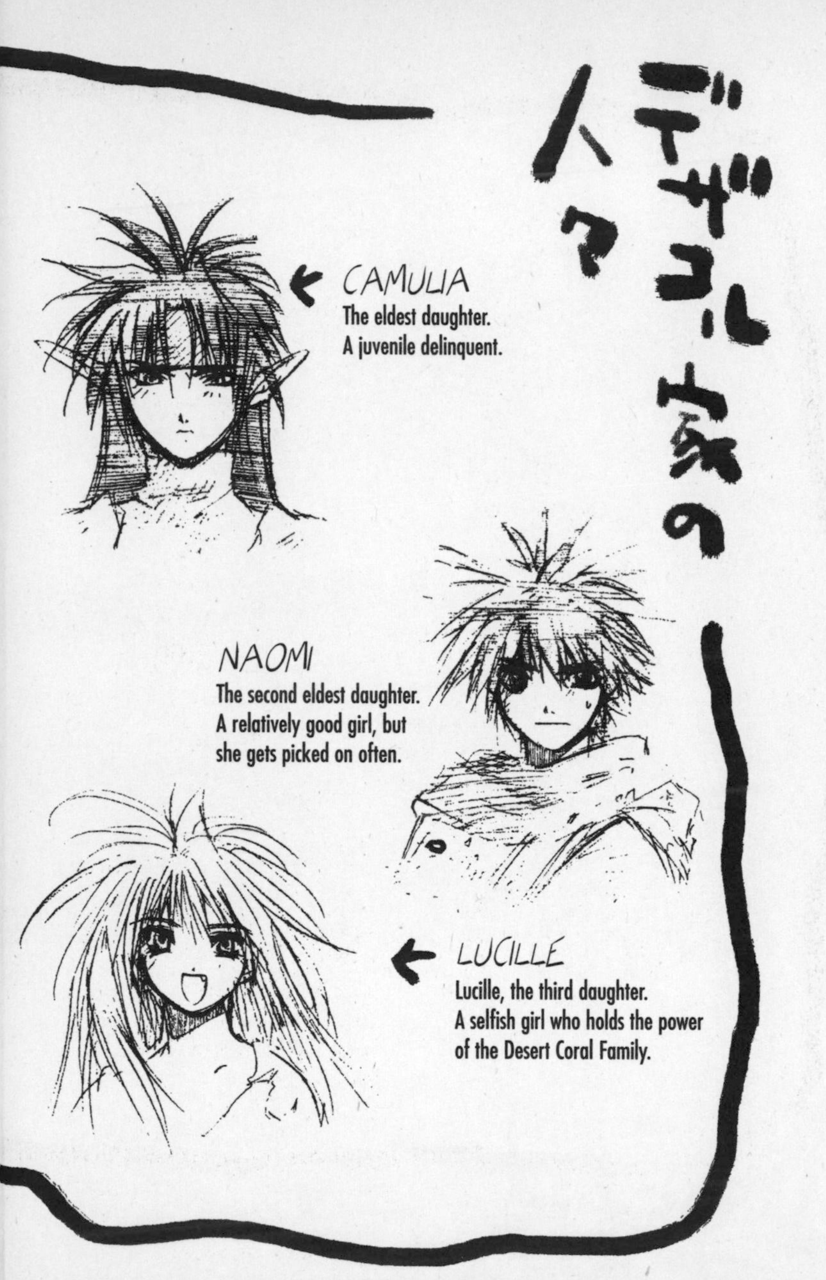

デザコール家の人々
CAMULIA
The eldest daughter.
A juvenile delinquent.
NAOMI
The second eldest daughter.
A relatively good girl, but
she gets picked on often.
LUCILLE
Lucille, the third daughter.
A selfish girl who holds the power
of the Desert Coral Family.

MEMBERS OF THE DESERT CORAL "FAMILY"

"She" gets mad if the kids don't come home before dinner time. Note the cat's ears.

A useless dad who has no interest in doing chores or taking care of the kids.

She can tell who has the weakest position within a family. She's well-behaved in front of outsiders.

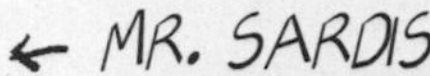

A perverted neighbor who follows Lucille and the pet around.

DESERT CORAL VOLUME TWO

First published in 2003 by Mag Garden Co., Ltd., Tokyo, Japan.
English translation rights arranged with Mag Garden Co., Ltd.

Translator	EIKO MCGREGOR
Lead Translator/TranslationSupervisor	JAVIER LOPEZ
ADV Manga Translation Staff	JOSH COLE, BRENDAN FRAYNE, AMY FORSYTH, KAY BERTRAND, HARUKA KANEKO-SMITH, MADOKA MOROE
Print Production/ Art Studio Manager	LISA PUCKETT
Pre-press Manager	KLYS REEDYK
Art Production Manager	RYAN MASON
Sr. Designer/Creative Manager	JORGE ALVARADO
Graphic Designer/Group Leader	SCOTT SAVAGE
Graphic Designer	NATALIA MORALES
Graphic Artists	CHRIS LAPP, CHY LING, LISA RAPER & NANAKO TSUKIHASHI
Graphic Intern	MARK MEZA
International Coordinator	TORU IWAKAMI
International Coordinator	ATSUSHI KANBAYASHI
Publishing Editor	SUSAN ITIN
Assistant Editor	MARGARET SCHAROLD
Editorial Assistant	VARSHA BHUCHAR
Proofreaders	SHERIDAN JACOBS, STEVEN REED
Research/ Traffic Coordinator	MARSHA ARNOLD
Excecutive, VP, CFO, COO	KEVIN CORCORAN
President, CEO & Publisher	JOHN LEDFORD

Email: editor@adv-manga.com
www.adv-manga.com
www.advfilms.com

For sales and distribution inquiries please call 1.800.282.7202

ADV Manga™ is a division of A.D. Vision, Inc.
10114 W. Sam Houston Parkway, Suite 200, Houston, Texas 77099

ISBN: 1-4139-0088-7
First printing, August 2004
10 9 8 7 6 5 4 3 2 1
Printed in Canada

LETTER FROM THE
ADV MANGA
TRANSLATION STAFF

Dear Reader,

On behalf of the ADV Manga translation team, thank you for purchasing an ADV book. We are enthusiastic and committed to our work, and strive to carry our enthusiasm over into the book you hold in your hands.

Our goal is to retain the spirit of the original Japanese book. While great care has been taken to render a true and accurate translation, some cultural or readability issues may require a line to be adapted for greater accessibility to our readers. At times, manga titles that include culturally-specific concepts will feature a "Translator's Notes" section, which explains noteworthy references to the original text.

We hope our commitment to a faithful translation is evident in every ADV book you purchase.

Sincerely,

Javier Lopez
Lead Translator

Madoka Moroe

Haruka Kaneko-Smith

Eiko McGregor

Kay Bertrand

Brendan Frayne

Amy Forsyth

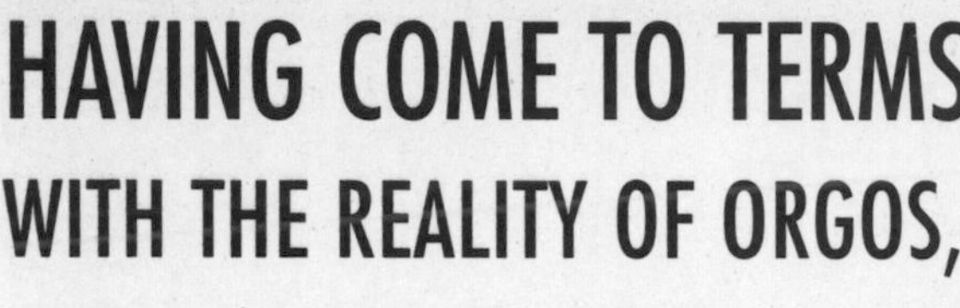

HAVING COME TO TERMS WITH THE REALITY OF ORGOS,

NAOTO FINDS HIMSELF COMPELLED TO STAY

AND FIGHT THE ELPHIS AS A MEMBER OF DESERT CORAL.

HIS BOND WITH LUSIA REVEALED THE DANGERS HE FACES, AS A BURNING FEVER NEARLY TAKES HIM DOWN AND OUT—BUT THAT'S ONLY PART OF THE TRIAL THAT HE MUST FACE IN HIS TRAINING IN THE ART OF SORCERY. STILL, NAOTO FINDS HIS OWN PRESENCE A MYSTERY IN THE WORLD OF ORGOS. WHEN HE AWAKENS TO MEMORIES OF HIS PAST, HE WILL FIND HIMSELF CAUGHT BETWEEN WORLDS. WHAT CHOICES WILL NAOTO HAVE TO MAKE? FIND OUT, AS THE ADVENTURE CONTINUES IN...

Available November 2004

EDITOR'S
PICKS

IF YOU LIKED DESERT CORAL VOLUME 2, THEN YOU'LL LOVE THESE!

PICK 1

BLUE INFERIOR

In a post-apocalyptic world, whatever life has survived subsists only in small pockets throughout the world. Existence is somewhat carefree, but certain fears obstruct complete happiness—fear of the outside world, the unknown, the stories about the subhumans. These creatures threaten entire populations, making the people quite unwelcoming to newcomers. A young girl with amnesia—Marine—who washes up on shore one day, is no exception to their apprehension. It is only through the kindness of a boy named Kazuya that Marine will be able to escape the hostile town and find out who she really is.

PICK 2

ARIA

After moving to the planet Aqua (formerly Mars), Akari Mizunashi has made her home in the charming town of Neo-Venezia, a reproduction of the ancient Earth city of Venice. Determined to become an undine, Akari spends her days training in the labyrinths of canals throughout the city, and finding fascinating adventures within her new, intriguing planet. She enjoys the primitive lifestyle of her ancestors and has no qualms about doing her own laundry or cooking meals from scratch, and she even enjoys scraping barnacles off of her boat! Pursuing this career and becoming independent are her dreams and, with the help of some curious Martians, underground dwellers and even wild creatures, Akari will one day captain her own gondola through the city of Neo-Venezia.

PICK 3

R²

Life for Kenta Akagi is safe, stable and altogether uneventful. Born and raised in the remote city of Lutzheim, he can only wonder what strange and wonderful creatures exist, or how battles are fought and won. A life of excitement is unknown to young Kenta, until he is whisked away to a foreign land. He becomes a warrior, fighting for possession of a girl, but he doesn't know who or what this girl is. He only senses that he must protect her, even if it causes more destruction than peace...

CHECK'EM OUT TODAY!

www.adv-manga.com

LOOKING FOR
ANIME NETWORK?

THIS GUY WAS, THEN HE CALLED HIS LOCAL
CABLE PROVIDER AND DEMANDED HIS ANIME!

FOR MORE INFO LOG ON TO
WWW.THEANIMENETWORK.COM

ANIME
NETWORK

ANIME • MANGA • VIDEO GAMES • TOYS • MOVIES •
IF IT'S COOL, YOU'LL FIND IT EACH AND EVERY MONTH IN THE PAGES OF NEWTYPE USA, ALONG WITH FREE DVDS, POSTERS, POST-CARDS AND MUCH, MUCH MORE. SUBSCRIBE TODAY! GO TO WWW.NEWTYPE-USA.COM
Newtype USA 米国版
THE MOVING PICTURES MAGAZINE.
月刊ニュータイプ
IT BEGINS WHERE OTHER MAGAZINES END •